NATIONAL GEOGRAPHIC

T0308155

Pirate TALES

PIONEER EDITION

By Francis Downey and Sara Lorimer

CONTENTS

Pirate King

Scientists Search for the Real Blackbeard

By Francis Downey

SCIENTISTS HAVE FOUND a sunken treasure off the North Carolina coast. It's not a pirate's treasure. But it may be a pirate ship.

Scientists think they have found Blackbeard's ship. He was a famous pirate. His ship, the *Queen Anne's Revenge*, sank in 1718. Since then, the ship has been lost to history.

Now that's changing. A bell and some cannons have been brought up. Part of the ship's hull, or body, has been brought up, too. The objects are helping scientists learn about life on a pirate ship. Let's sail with Blackbeard and his **crew**. What were their lives like?

BLACKBEARD KNEW how to impress people. A large black beard covered his face. He may have put lit candles under his hat. People saw flames around his face. Smoke circled his head. It looked like he was on fire.

Sea Sagas

There were many amazing stories about Blackbeard's adventures. Some were true. Many were made up. Despite these tales, little is known about him.

Historians don't even know Blackbeard's real name. This isn't surprising. Many pirates made up their names.

All the records from Blackbeard's time call him Blackbeard or Edward Teach. His name was also spelled Thatch, Thack, or Thatche.

Finding Blackbeard

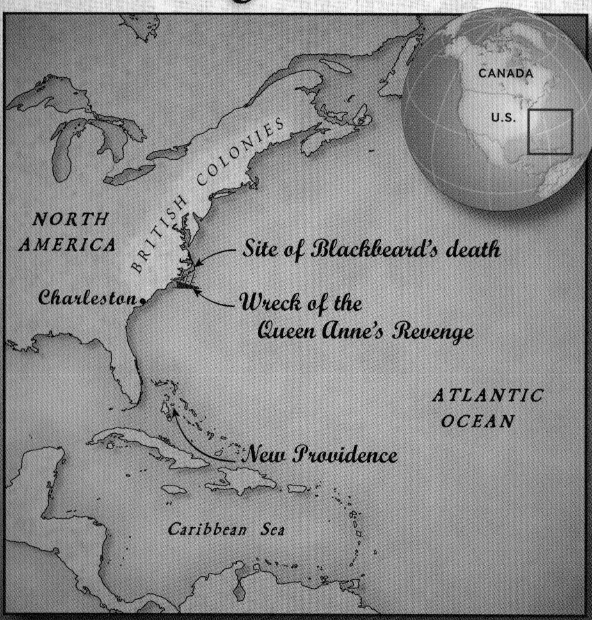

Teach's Teacher

No one really even knows where Blackbeard was born. Most say he was born in England. Some say he was born in America.

In 1716, Blackbeard probably was on a small island called New Providence. There he met Captain Benjamin Hornigold. Hornigold was a pirate **captain**.

Blackbeard may have joined Hornigold's crew. If so, they set out for adventure. Blackbeard learned a lot from his teacher. He became a good pirate. So Hornigold gave Blackbeard a ship.

Pirate Plunder

The next year, Blackbeard spotted a ship in the distance. His crew got ready to fight. They raised the pirate flag. Pirate flags were usually black. The most famous had a skull and crossbones. It's called the Jolly Roger.

When they got near the ship, they fired at it. The other ship stopped fighting quickly. The ship was now pirate plunder. Blackbeard renamed the ship *Queen Anne's Revenge*, after a queen of England.

Unwanted Guests. *Smoke rises from a damaged ship. Pirates get ready to come on board.*

A Pirate's Life

It wasn't easy being a pirate captain. True, captains were in charge of their ships. But they were not dictators. Their crews elected them. Captains had to be brave, smart, and mean. If they weren't, their crews would replace them.

Life for a pirate crew wasn't easy either. They lived and worked on a ship's deck. Often, they didn't have enough food or water. Many got sick.

Pirates had to follow the pirate code. If they broke a rule, punishments were harsh. Pirates never walked the plank. That's just a myth. However, some were tied, tossed into the water, and dragged behind the ship.

Crew members came from many different countries. Still, they had things in common. They all wanted to get rich. They were all criminals.

Port of Call

Pirate attacks weren't always about money. In a famous adventure in 1718, Blackbeard sailed to Charleston, South Carolina. He took several prisoners. He threatened to kill them unless the townspeople gave him medicine. The people were scared. So they gave him the medicine.

In less than two years, Blackbeard had attacked a town. He had captured more than 50 ships. Then Blackbeard decided to stop being a pirate. He sank his ship off North Carolina. Then the governor of North Carolina **pardoned** him for his crimes.

Blackbeard now led the life of a gentleman. He dined with the governor of North Carolina. He married the daughter of a wealthy farmer. Many people respected him.

A Pirate's End

Yet a quiet life wasn't really what Blackbeard wanted. He soon got together with some of his old crew. They went on pirate raids again.

These plundering pirate raids didn't last long. Pirates made enemies—lots of enemies.

The governor of Virginia was one of Blackbeard's enemies. He sent a crew to kill Blackbeard. They found him on a ship with his old pirate crew. They attacked and killed him. Blackbeard soon joined many other pirates at the bottom of the ocean.

The career of a pirate was short. Most only lasted at sea for two or three years. Blackbeard was no different. Yet his legend lives on. Today, many people think of him and other pirates as heroes. At the time, most sailors feared them. Pirates were the scariest criminals of their time.

Wordwise

captain: the person in charge of a ship

crew: the people who work on a ship

pardon: let go without punishment

Fact or Fiction?
Did Blackbeard really have his men bury treasure? No one knows.

BRINGING UP PIRATE BOUNTY

ON THE NIGHT of April 26, 1717, a ship sailed past Cape Cod, Massachusetts. Then it ran into a dangerous storm. The ship was called the *Whydah Galley*. The storm hurt the ship and it sank.

The ship sat on the bottom of the ocean for 267 years. In July 1984, researchers found the ship.

To learn more about life on the *Whydah*, scientists study artifacts from the ship. They use underwater archaeology to bring up the artifacts.

The archaeologists wear heavy air tanks. The tanks give them air to breathe under water. The tanks also make their work hard and slow. Find out what other challenges they face.

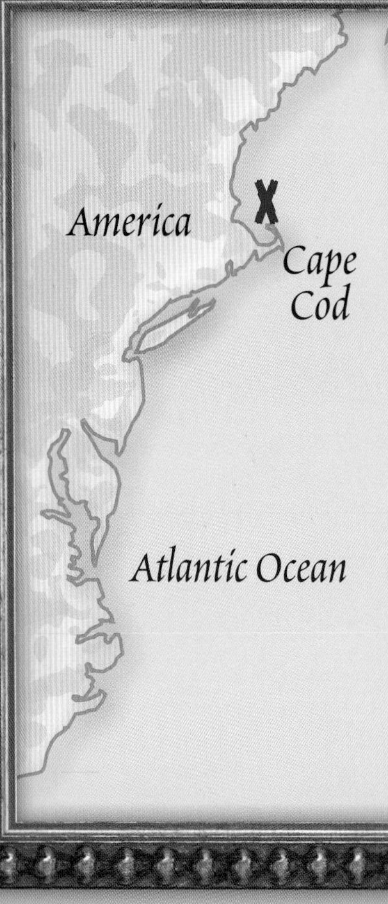

THE TALE OF BLACK SAM BELLAMY

"Black Sam" Bellamy was an English pirate. When he started his pirate career, he sailed with Captain Benjamin Hornigold. Blackbeard probably sailed with them, too!

In 1716, Sam became a pirate captain. He and his crew attacked many ships.

In February 1717, Sam captured the *Whydah Galley*. The ship was loaded with gold. Sam took over the ship. Then he sailed to Cape Cod.

These gold coins and jewelry are treasures from the Whydah.

How do archaeologists find artifacts? Here, a person uses a light and a metal detector (right). This equipment makes it easier to find small metal objects from the *Whydah.*

How do archaeologists dig up artifacts? They carefully brush away the sand. This is a part of the *Whydah*'s hull, or body.

How do archaeologists bring artifacts up from the water? They attach ropes and airbags. As the bags float up, they lift the artifact to the surface, too. This person watches a small cannon from the *Whydah* rise to the surface.

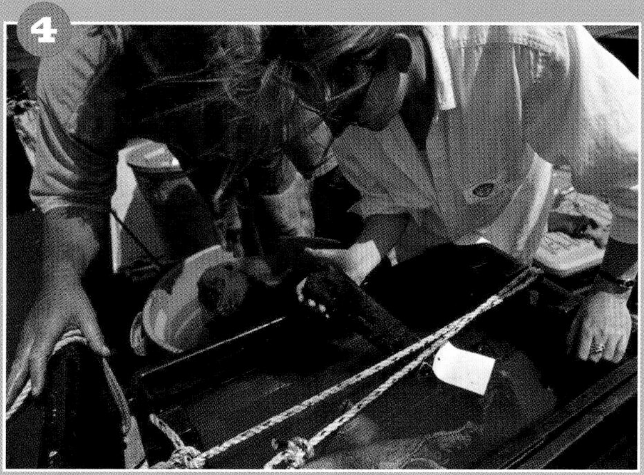

How do archaeologists protect artifacts? They store them in buckets of water. This keeps them from drying out. This person studies a piece of wood from the *Whydah.*

Girl Pirate

By Sara Lorimer

Some pirates were girls and women. Piracy gave women freedoms they did not have on land. Plus, they did not have to run a house or support a family. At sea, a pirate woman kept her own hours. She spent them drinking, gambling, and plundering!

Mary Read and Anne Bonney

WHERE AND WHEN: THE CARIBBEAN, EARLY 1700S

X After Mary Read's husband died, she needed money. So she got a job as a sailor on a ship. When the ship reached the Caribbean, pirates took it over. They gave Mary a choice. She could join up or be killed.

Strong Fighter. *Mary Read fights a duel and wins.*

So Mary became a pirate. She was good at dueling. That means fighting with weapons. One time, she thought that her boyfriend on the ship would be killed in a duel. So Mary picked a fight with the challenger. They had a duel. Mary won.

Mary met Anne Bonney. Anne had run away to sea with a pirate named Calico Jack. Both women were on Jack's ship. The three pirates attacked other boats. They mostly stole fishing gear and food. Even though their crimes were small, the English government condemned them. They said Jack and the women were enemies of Great Britain!

Rachel Wall

WHERE AND WHEN:
NEW ENGLAND COAST, LATE 1700S

Rachel Wall worked with her husband and a crew off the coast of Maine. After storms, they anchored their boat. They raised a distress flag. Rachel screamed. When people came to help, they were attacked!

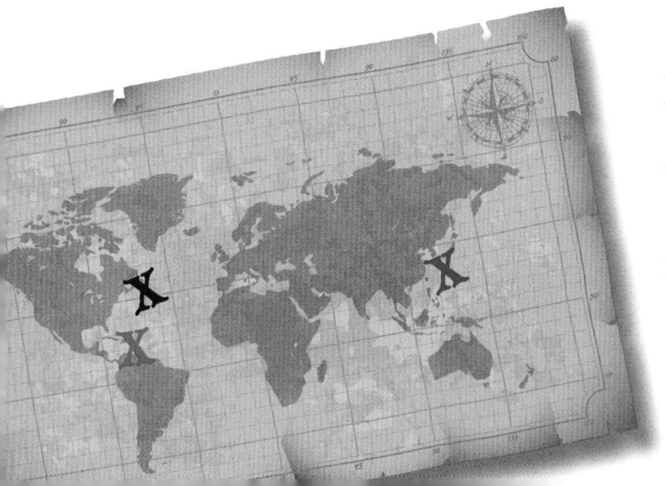

In two summers, Rachel and her husband probably killed 24 men. They stole $6,000. They took many valuable goods.

Cheng I Sao

WHERE AND WHEN:
SOUTH CHINA SEA, 1801–1810

Perhaps the greatest pirate of all time was Cheng I Sao. She ruled a fleet of 2,000 ships in the South China Sea. Madame Cheng turned to crime when she married a famous pirate. More than 80,000 pirates followed her commands. They took loot in many ways. They sold "protection" from pirate attacks. They raided ships. They kidnapped. Madame Cheng paid her pirates cash for the prizes they brought back!

CRIME DOESN'T PAY. Or does it? Mary Read and Anne Bonney were captured in 1720. Mary died in prison. What happened to Anne is a mystery. Eventually the law caught up with Rachel Wall, too. In 1789, she was hanged in Massachusetts. But the government could not stop Madame Cheng. Some say that after she retired from piracy, she became a smuggler. She died peacefully at age 69.

Pirate Treasure

Discover your own pirate riches. Then answer these questions.

1. What have scientists found off the coast of North Carolina? What will scientists learn from this find?

2. How did Blackbeard become a pirate? List the events in order.

3. What was Blackbeard's life like after he stopped being a pirate? Why did he become a pirate again?

4. Why is it hard for archaeologists to work underwater?

5. Why did some women become pirates?